THE SATURDAY EVENING POST
Spot the Differences
PICTURE PUZZLES

Photo alterations by Sara Jackson

DOVER PUBLICATIONS
Garden City, New York

The Saturday Evening Post Spot the Differences Picture Puzzles is a
new work, first published by Dover Publications in 2018.

ISBN-13: 978-0-486-81912-9
ISBN-10: 0-486-81912-4

Printed in China
81912411   2024
www.doverpublications.com

Inside this book, you will find twenty-five spot-the-difference challenges, featuring two brightly colored pictures of the same image. However, the one on the left features an accurate reproduction of an iconic cover from *The Saturday Evening Post*, while the page on the right has 11 to 15 changes for you to find. Try your best to complete each puzzle on your own—check boxes are provided to help you track your progress. If you get stuck, turn to the Solutions section, which begins on page 54.

Milkman Meets Pieman

Stevan Dohanos • *The Saturday Evening Post* cover, October 11, 1958
Illustration © SEPS. Licensed by Curtis Licensing, Indianapolis, Indiana

Hardware Store at Springtime

Stevan Dohanos • *The Saturday Evening Post* cover, March 16, 1946

Candidate Clash
Benjamin Prins • *The Saturday Evening Post* cover, November 12, 1955
Illustration © SEPS. Licensed by Curtis Licensing, Indianapolis, Indiana

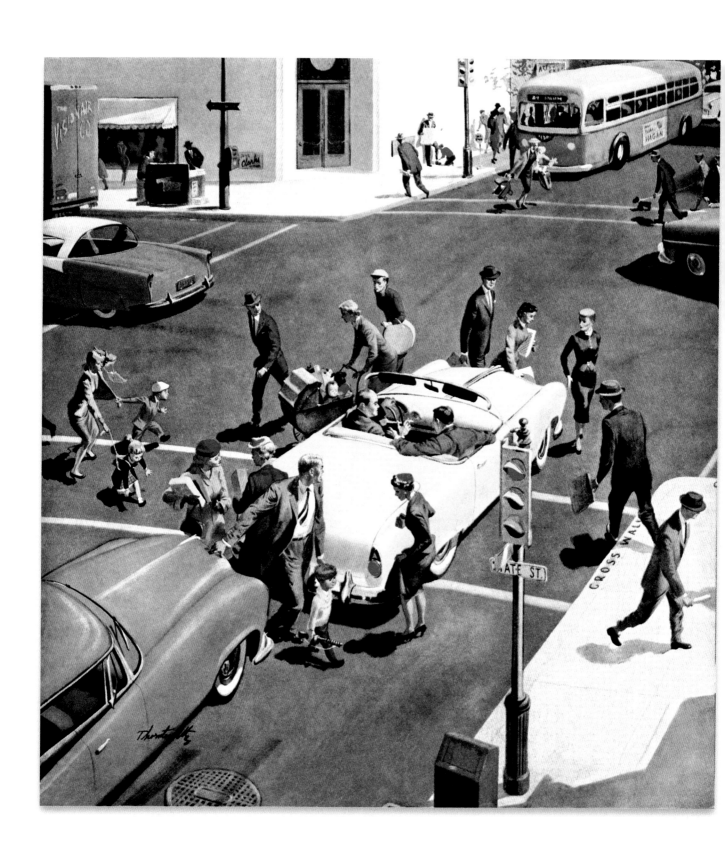

Blocking the Crosswalk
Thornton Utz • *The Saturday Evening Post* cover, September 17, 1955
Illustration © SEPS. Licensed by Curtis Licensing, Indianapolis, Indiana

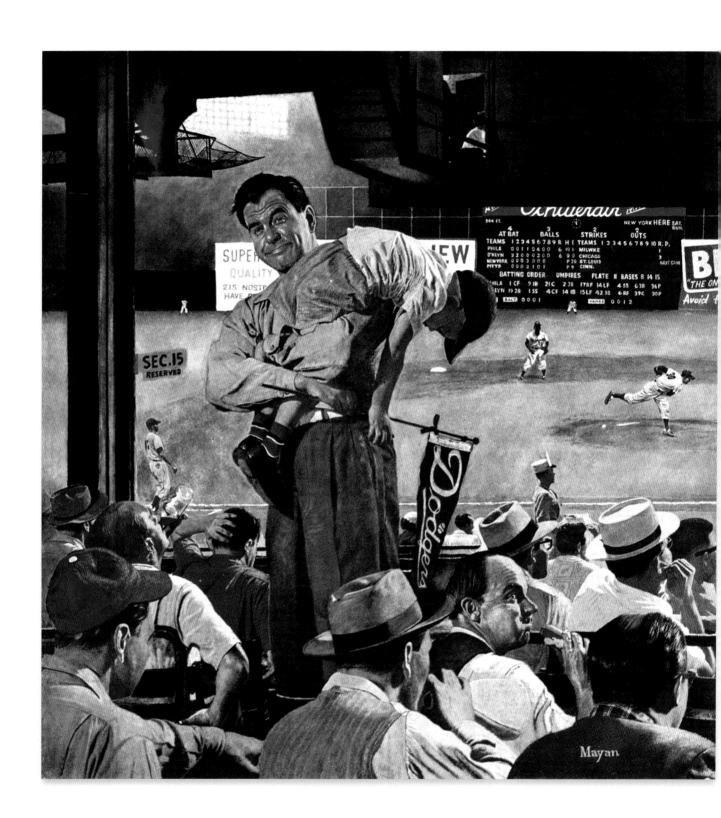

Sleepy Inning
Earl Mayan • *The Saturday Evening Post* cover, April 23, 1955
Illustration © SEPS. Licensed by Curtis Licensing, Indianapolis, Indiana

Road Block
Norman Rockwell • *The Saturday Evening Post* cover, July 9, 1949
Illustration © Rockwell Family Agency, Inc.

Sunscreen?
Kurt Ard • *The Saturday Evening Post* cover, August 16, 1958
Illustration © SEPS. Licensed by Curtis Licensing, Indianapolis, Indiana

King of the Beach
J. C. Leyendecker • *The Saturday Evening Post* cover, September 3, 1932
Illustration © SEPS. Licensed by Curtis Licensing, Indianapolis, Indiana

Hunting His Tux for the Party
Richard Sargent • *The Saturday Evening Post* cover, March 31, 1962
Illustration © SEPS. Licensed by Curtis Licensing, Indianapolis, Indiana

Penny Candy
Stevan Dohanos • *The Saturday Evening Post* cover, September 23, 1944
Illustration © SEPS. Licensed by Curtis Licensing, Indianapolis, Indiana

Returning Home from College
Stevan Dohanos • *The Saturday Evening Post* cover, June 5, 1948
Illustration © SEPS. Licensed by Curtis Licensing, Indianapolis, Indiana

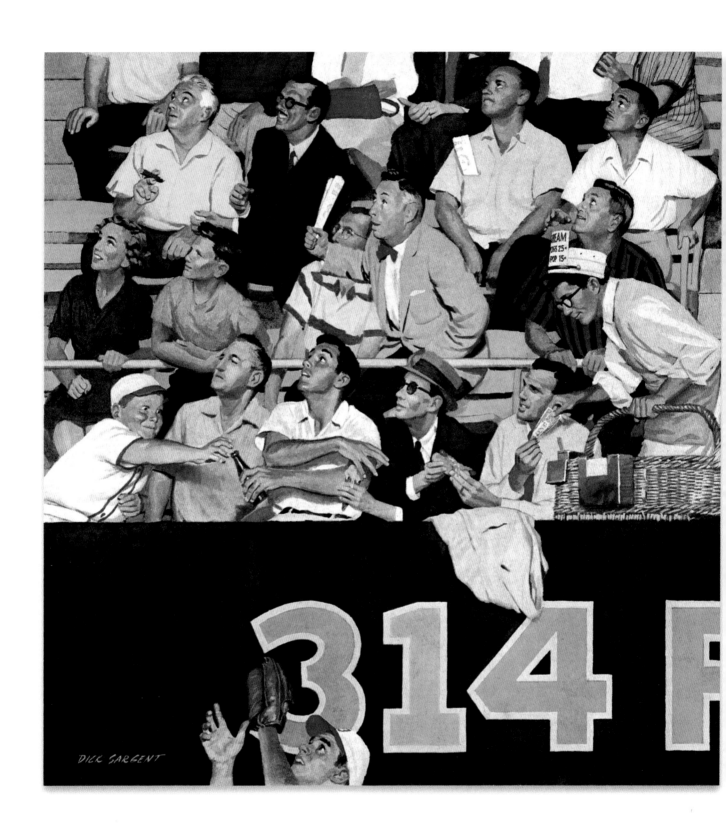

No Time for a Hotdog
Richard Sargent • *The Saturday Evening Post* cover, April 11, 1959
Illustration © SEPS. Licensed by Curtis Licensing, Indianapolis, Indiana

Wrong Week at the Ski Resort

James Williamson • *The Saturday Evening Post* cover, January 14, 1961
Illustration © SEPS. Licensed by Curtis Licensing, Indianapolis, Indiana

Bus Stop at Christmas
Stevan Dohanos • *The Saturday Evening Post* cover, December 13, 1952
Illustration © SEPS. Licensed by Curtis Licensing, Indianapolis, Indiana

Baby Sitter
Norman Rockwell • *The Saturday Evening Post* cover, November 8, 1947
Illustration © Rockwell Family Agency, Inc.

Keep Score: 13 Changes ■ ■ ■ ■ ■ ■ ■ ■ ■ ■ ■ ■ ■

Putting Around in the Kitchen
Richard Sargent • *The Saturday Evening Post* cover, September 3, 1960
Illustration © SEPS. Licensed by Curtis Licensing, Indianapolis, Indiana

Broken Antique Chair
John Falter • *The Saturday Evening Post* cover, June 20, 1959
Illustration © SEPS. Licensed by Curtis Licensing, Indianapolis, Indiana

Billboard Painters
Stevan Dohanos • *The Saturday Evening Post* cover, July 13, 1957
Illustration © SEPS. Licensed by Curtis Licensing, Indianapolis, Indiana

Packing the Car
Stevan Dohanos • *The Saturday Evening Post* cover, September 8, 1956
Illustration © SEPS. Licensed by Curtis Licensing, Indianapolis, Indiana

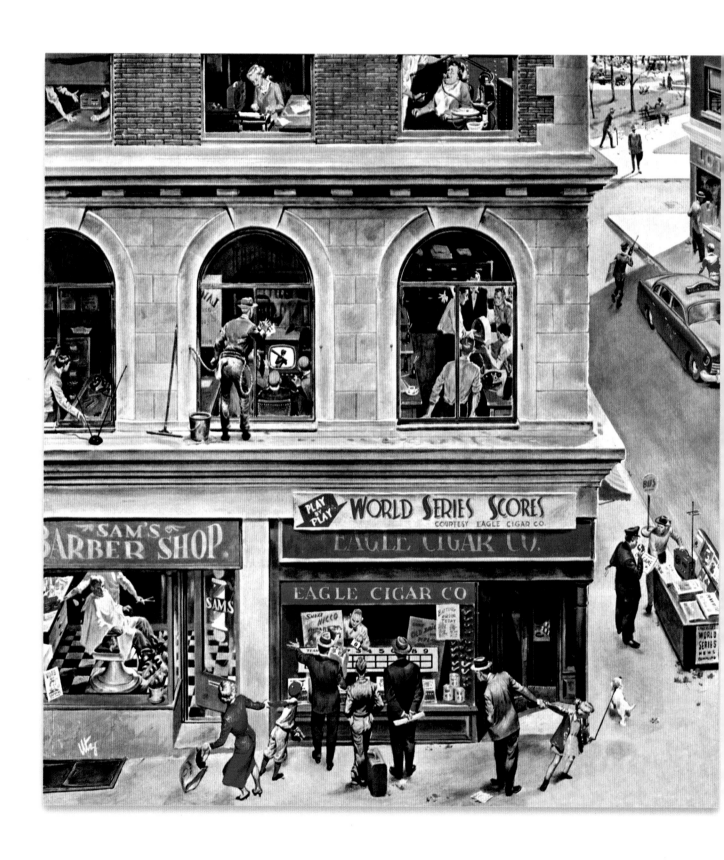

World Series Scores
Thornton Utz • *The Saturday Evening Post* cover, October 2, 1954
Illustration © SEPS. Licensed by Curtis Licensing, Indianapolis, Indiana

Home Improvement
Stevan Dohanos • *The Saturday Evening Post* cover, December 5, 1953
Illustration © SEPS. Licensed by Curtis Licensing, Indianapolis, Indiana

Mother's Little Helpers
John Falter • *The Saturday Evening Post* cover, April 18, 1953
Illustration © SEPS. Licensed by Curtis Licensing, Indianapolis, Indiana

Washington Crossing the Delaware
Stevan Dohanos • *The Saturday Evening Post* cover, February 24, 1951
Illustration © SEPS. Licensed by Curtis Licensing, Indianapolis, Indiana

Coastal Post Office
Stevan Dohanos • *The Saturday Evening Post* cover, August 26, 1950
Illustration © SEPS. Licensed by Curtis Licensing, Indianapolis, Indiana

April Fool, 1943
Norman Rockwell • *The Saturday Evening Post* cover, April 3, 1943
Illustration © Rockwell Family Agency, Inc.

Solutions

Pages 4 – 5

1. Handle added
2. Pencil removed
3. Pie piece changed
4. Letter on truck changed
5. Chimney removed
6. Sunglasses added
7. Jar of milk changed
8. Cat's eyes added
9. Sun decal added
10. Sock color changed
11. Pie changed
12. Snake added

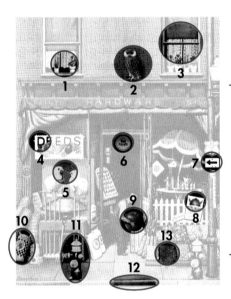

Pages 6 – 7

1. Plant removed
2. Owl added
3. Shade moved up
4. Letter changed
5. Length of worm changed
6. Sign shape changed
7. Arrow direction changed
8. Sign changed
9. Flowers changed
10. Color of bag changed
11. Fire hydrant added
12. Color of curb changed
13. Flowers removed

Pages 8 – 9

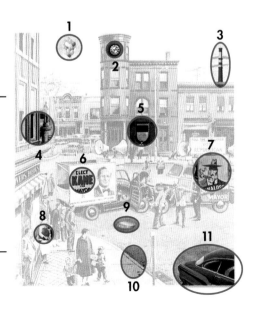

1. Balloons added
2. Clock face changed
3. Smokestack added
4. Man in window removed
5. Window upside down
6. Name changed
7. Photo changed
8. Groceries changed
9. Manhole cover changed
10. Fire hydrant removed
11. Car color changed

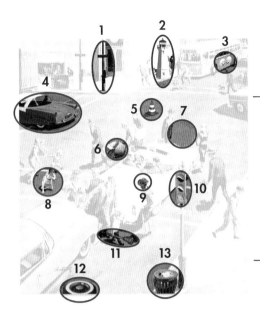

Pages 10 – 11

1. Street pole added
2. Street light changed
3. Bus advertisement changed
4. Car color changed
5. Street cone added
6. Carriage occupants changed
7. Woman removed
8. Toddler changed
9. Woman's hat changed
10. Traffic light changed
11. Child's toy changed
12. Manhole cover changed
13. Trash can changed

Pages 12 – 13

1. Light added
2. Stadium background changed
3. Section number changed
4. Hat color changed
5. Letter changed
6. Pitcher position changed
7. Megaphone added
8. Mustard stain added
9. Vendor changed
10. Earphones added
11. Hotdog changed

Pages 14 – 15

1. Poster changed
2. Sign changed
3. Bird removed
4. Shape on truck changed
5. T-shirt design added
6. Graffiti added
7. Paintbrush changed
8. Truck window changed
9. Man's hat changed
10. License plate changed
11. Number on truck door changed
12. Backpack changed
13. Man's arm removed
14. Hat color changed

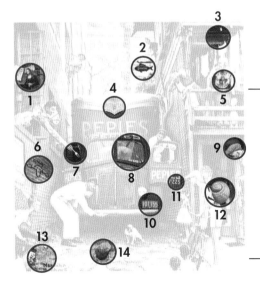

Pages 16 – 17

1. Lipstick color changed
2. Extra hand added
3. Radio changed
4. Bottle added
5. Book changed
6. Newspaper copy changed
7. Stack of gold coins added
8. Design added to bag
9. Magazine photo changed
10. Sea crab added
11. Shell added
12. Man's foot removed

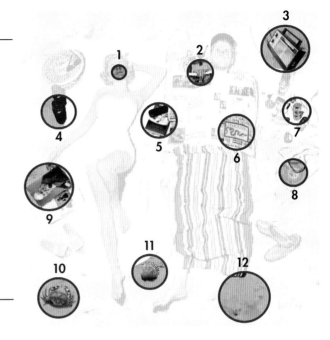

Pages 18 – 19

1. Sunglasses added
2. Bathing suit changed
3. Belt changed
4. Beach ball changed
5. Tattoo added
6. Life preserver changed
7. Box of treats removed
8. Dog's stick changed
9. Playing cards added
10. Person's foot removed
11. Bathing suit color changed
12. Shark fin added
13. Pail changed

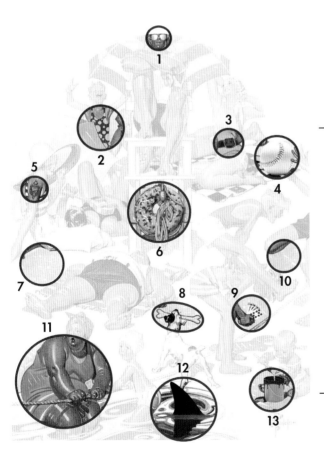

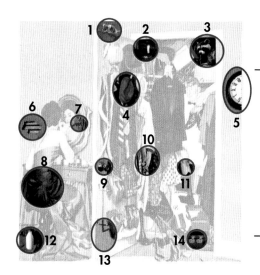

Pages 20 – 21

1. Mouse added
2. Football added
3. Raccoon added
4. Hat color changed
5. Wall hanging changed
6. Hole in wall added
7. Earring in mirror changed
8. Color of dress sash changed
9. Doorknob added
10. Hand added
11. Sock garter removed
12. Milk bottle added
13. Hanging sock removed
14. Suitcase hardware added

Pages 22 – 23

1. Electric light added
2. Bottle added
3. Eyeglasses added
4. Cone of twine changed
5. Number on cash register changed
6. Photo on calendar changed
7. Contents of jar changed
8. Hat added
9. Electrical outlet added
10. Hole in shirt removed
11. Contents of box changed
12. Coin in hand changed
13. Bird added
14. Soda bottle contents changed
15. Striped sock added

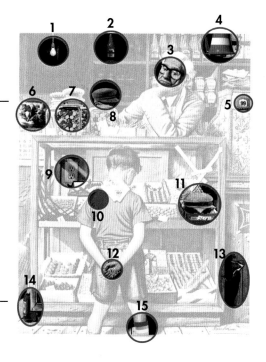

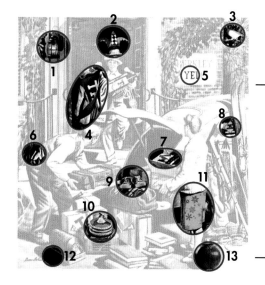

Pages 24 – 25

1. Light added
2. Top hat changed
3. Security camera added
4. Banner color changed
5. Word changed
6. Pocket handkerchief changed
7. Book cover changed
8. Sign on car window added
9. Baseball cleats changed
10. Record player turntable changed
11. Skirt color changed
12. Baseball removed
13. Basketball replaced

Pages 26 – 27

1. Foam finger added
2. Drink added
3. Newspaper changed
4. Paper added to pocket
5. Person changed
6. Flower added
7. Hat sign removed
8. Shirt color changed
9. Hand removed
10. Drink bottle changed
11. Jacket added
12. Hotdog changed
13. Cat added
14. Hand changed
15. Space in number removed

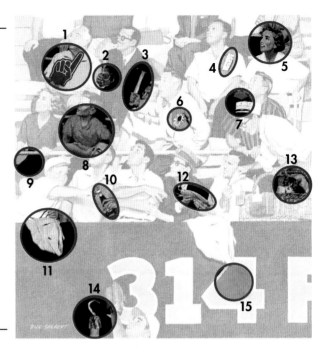

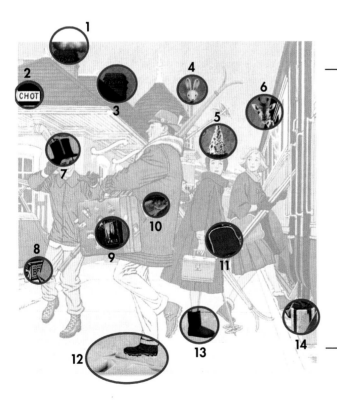

Pages 28 – 29

1. Smoke added
2. Letters changed
3. Chimney added
4. Train signal changed
5. Party hat added
6. Giraffe added
7. Hat changed
8. License plate changed
9. Decal changed
10. Fish added
11. Writing on bag changed
12. Sidewalk crack added
13. Boots changed
14. Gift added

Pages 30 – 31

1. Cane removed
2. Words on sign changed
3. Funny face glasses added
4. Address number added
5. Package removed
6. Red ornament added
7. Scarf color changed
8. Gloved hand added
9. Santa Claus decal added
10. Ribbon decoration added
11. Sewer grate added
12. Duck changed
13. Window decal added to gift box

Pages 32 – 33

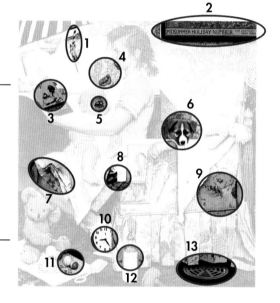

1. Straw added
2. Artwork changed
3. Book cover changed
4. Length of hair removed
5. Teeth added
6. Puppy added
7. Color on skirt hemline changed
8. Pencil removed
9. Chair design changed
10. Time on clock changed
11. Toy added
12. Milk in bottle changed
13. Floor grate added

Pages 34 – 35

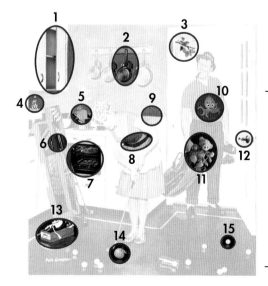

1. Cabinet door opened
2. Pans added
3. Tree branch added
4. Candle added
5. Spaghetti added
6. Card removed
7. Oven door changed
8. Belt added
9. Bottle removed
10. Design on shirt added
11. Teddy bear added
12. Doorknob changed
13. Box color changed
14. Golf ball changed
15. Golf ball added

Pages 36 – 37

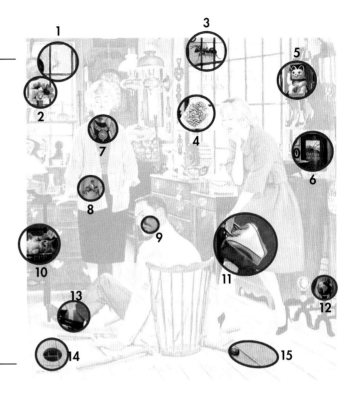

1. Pan removed
2. Flowers added
3. Bug added
4. Lamp shade design changed
5. Lucky Cat figurine added
6. Framed print changed
7. Necklace changed
8. Pocket frog added
9. Pipe removed
10. Cat added
11. Handbag changed
12. Ornament changed
13. Sock color changed
14. Hole in floor added
15. Section of chair leg removed

Pages 38 – 39

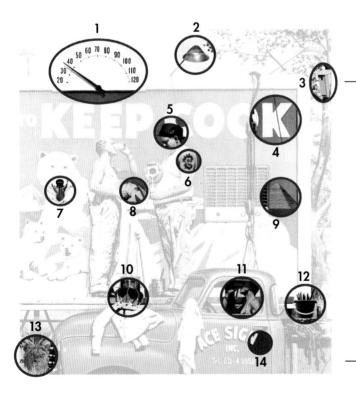

1. Temperature changed
2. Light fixture changed
3. Birdhouse added
4. Letter changed
5. Man's hat changed
6. Tattoo added
7. Polar bear's tongue added
8. Paintbrush changed
9. Mountain on billboard changed
10. Hat on top of truck changed
11. Man in truck added
12. Paint bucket changed
13. Lion added
14. Letter "S" removed

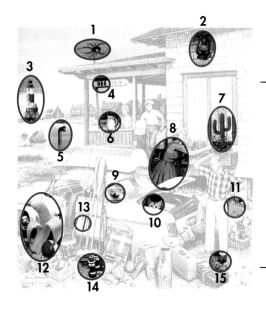

Pages 40 – 41

1. Fish ornament changed
2. Lantern added
3. Lighthouse added
4. Word changed
5. Periscope added
6. Bottle of milk changed
7. Cactus added
8. Color of dress changed
9. Decal added
10. Cat added
11. Baseball cap removed
12. Water float changed
13. Revolver on pole removed
14. Lantern added
15. Sneaker changed

Pages 42 – 43

1. Bricks changed
2. Jack-o'-lantern added
3. Building light added
4. Window flag added
5. Man removed
6. Bucket removed
7. Gargoyle added
8. Manhole cover added
9. Name on sign changed
10. Letter "L" removed
11. Radio color changed
12. Shopping bag removed
13. Vintage baseball poster added
14. Dog changed

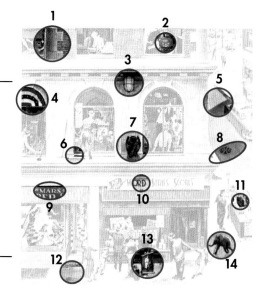

Pages 44 – 45

1. Artwork changed
2. Paintbrush changed
3. Fire extinguishers added
4. Glass light shade removed
5. Electrical outlet removed
6. Flamingo head added
7. Mustache added
8. Flowers added
9. Seat back color changed
10. Fruit changed
11. Glass of milk changed
12. Fried egg changed
13. Colander changed
14. Egg removed

Pages 46 – 47

1. Ceiling fan added
2. Chef hat changed
3. Person removed
4. Oven mitt color changed
5. Birdhouse added
6. Handprint added
7. Dog added
8. Syrup bottle changed
9. Emoji face added
10. Cotton candy added
11. Carton changed
12. Apple added
13. Pot changed
14. Broken egg removed

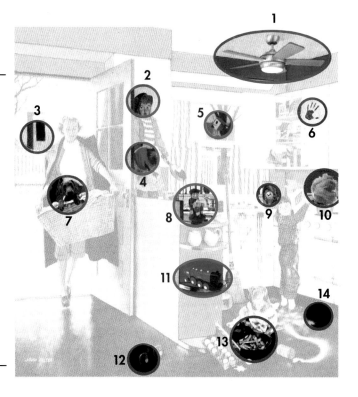

Pages 48 – 49

1. Airplane added
2. Windmill added
3. Washington's direction changed
4. Flag stars removed
5. Dragon added
6. Oar changed
7. Candy cane added
8. Soldier's arm removed
9. Soldier's hand removed
10. Girl's hat changed
11. Hat added
12. Handbag changed
13. Iceberg added
14. Skirt length changed
15. Coat color changed

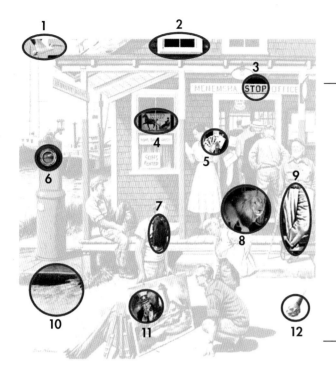

Pages 50 – 51

1. Seagull added
2. Window added
3. Word changed
4. Sign in window changed
5. Mail changed
6. Fuel gauge changed
7. Beard added
8. Dog on porch changed
9. Man's leg position changed
10. Black dog removed
11. Artwork changed
12. Ice cream cone added

Pages 52 – 53

1. Staircase decoration changed
2. Artwork changed
3. Clock face changed
4. Fingers removed from man in painting
5. Pencil behind the ear changed
6. Animal face in mantel changed
7. Contents of glass changed
8. Contents of pocket changed
9. Paper changed
10. Wrench removed
11. Little door added
12. Milk bottle changed
13. Wallet with cash changed
14. Deer's tongue added

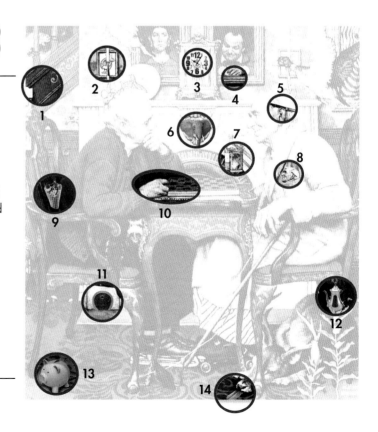